IT'S TIME TO EAT JACK FRUIT

It's Time to Eat JACK FRUIT

Walter the Educator

Silent King Books
A WhichHead Entertainment Imprint

Copyright © 2024 by Walter the Educator

All rights reserved. No part of this book may be reproduced in any manner whatsoever without written per- mission except in the case of brief quotations embodied in critical articles and reviews.

First Printing, 2024

Disclaimer

This book is a literary work; the story is not about specific persons, locations, situations, and/or circumstances unless mentioned in a historical context. Any resemblance to real persons, locations, situations, and/or circumstances is coincidental. This book is for entertainment and informational purposes only. The author and publisher offer this information without warranties expressed or implied. No matter the grounds, neither the author nor the publisher will be accountable for any losses, injuries, or other damages caused by the reader's use of this book. The use of this book acknowledges an understanding and acceptance of this disclaimer.

It's Time to Eat JACK FRUIT is a collectible early learning book by Walter the Educator suitable for all ages belonging to Walter the Educator's Time to Eat Book Series. Collect more books at WaltertheEducator.com

USE THE EXTRA SPACE TO TAKE NOTES AND DOCUMENT YOUR MEMORIES

JACK FRUIT

It's time to eat, hooray, hooray!

It's Time to Eat
Jack Fruit

The jackfruit's ripe and on display.

So big and bumpy, green and round,

The sweetest fruit that can be found.

We cut it open, what's inside?

A golden treasure, bright and wide.

The fruit is sticky, soft, and sweet,

A yummy snack that's fun to eat.

Its smell is bold, it fills the air,

A fruity treat beyond compare.

Each piece is like a golden sun,

Eating jackfruit is so much fun!

Pull out the pods, they're smooth and bright,

They taste like honey, pure delight.

One by one, or in a dish,

Jackfruit's flavor grants your wish.

It's Time to Eat
Jack Fruit

Make it a smoothie, or eat it plain,

This fruit is magic, it's hard to explain!

It's filling too, it's big and strong,

It keeps you going all day long.

The seeds inside, don't toss away,

You can cook them up another day.

Boil or roast, they're fun to try,

A hidden snack you can't deny!

The jackfruit grows on trees so tall,

The biggest fruit among them all.

Its weight is heavy, its size is grand,

A gift of nature's loving hand.

It comes from places warm and bright,

Where sunshine fills the days with light.

A fruit to share with family near,

It's Time to Eat
Jack Fruit

Jackfruit brings us joy and cheer.

So take a bite, let's shout hooray!

For jackfruit's goodness every day.

It's time to eat, come join the feast,

A golden fruit from west to east.

When you're done, save every seed,

And plant them where the soil's in need.

The tree will grow, so big and sweet,

It's Time to Eat
Jack Fruit

With jackfruit treats for all to eat!

ABOUT THE CREATOR

Walter the Educator is one of the pseudonyms for Walter Anderson. Formally educated in Chemistry, Business, and Education, he is an educator, an author, a diverse entrepreneur, and he is the son of a disabled war veteran. "Walter the Educator" shares his time between educating and creating. He holds interests and owns several creative projects that entertain, enlighten, enhance, and educate, hoping to inspire and motivate you. Follow, find new works, and stay up to date with Walter the Educator™ at WaltertheEducator.com

www.ingramcontent.com/pod-product-compliance
Lightning Source LLC
LaVergne TN
LVHW052012060526
838201LV00059B/4000